a gift for us to share

to:
....

from:
....

OTHER HELEN EXLEY GIFTBOOKS IN THIS SERIES:

Me and my Mum

Me and my Mom

Me and my Dad

Me and my Grandma

Me and my Grandpa

Me and my Teacher

OTHER HELEN EXLEY GIFTBOOKS:

Giggles: A Joke Book

Crazy Kids' Jokes

To a very special Friend

Published in 2006 by Helen Exley Giftbooks in Great Britain, and Helen Exley Giftbooks LLC in the USA.

12 11 10 9 8 7 6 5 4 3 2 1

Illustrations © Jane Massey 2006
Copyright © Helen Exley 2006
The moral right of the author has been asserted.

ISBN 1-905130-86-4

A copy of the CIP data is available from the British Library on request.

Printed in China

Helen Exley Giftbooks, 16 Chalk Hill, Watford, Herts WD19 4BG, UK,
Helen Exley Giftbooks LLC, 185 Main Street, Spencer MA 01562, USA.
www.helenexleygiftbooks.com

Written by Helen Exley and Illustrated by Jane Massey

Me
and my
Friend

This is me and my friend.

We go to the same school.

I used to feel lonely at school

and I didn't like going. But now I do.

I have a kind teacher

and I've found a best friend.

My friend Jamie and I go on picnics.
We take packed lunches
and always swap and
share our tastiest food.
And we laugh
and fool around.
We just seem
to like being together.

We talk all the time
about our plans and the great adventures
we're going to have together.
We just talk and talk and talk.

When you've got a friend

you don't feel alone.

If I see some exciting movie I just

have to call and tell Jamie about it...

I think it's wonderful when you've

got a best friend to share things with.

Wow! Can we eat cherries!

One day the DVD we were watching was so scary that we ate two bowls full of cherries and didn't even notice!

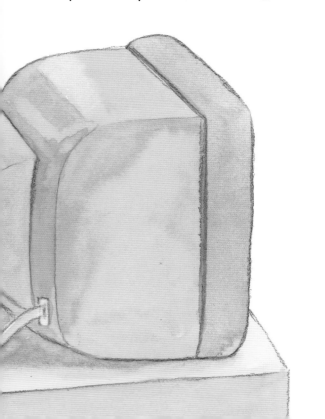

We always help each other.

Jamie holds the umbrella over me when it simply pours down. A friend shelters you; Jamie is my protector.

One day I was very upset and worried
because I really didn't Know
how to do my school homework.

My friend came round to help,

and was just there, quiet and kind.

Sometimes you don't have to talk

to understand when

you've got a best friend.

Sometimes my friend comes round
so that we can do our homework together.
Jamie teaches me history and I try to
show Jamie how to do the difficult sums.
And then we forget to do the homework...

One time we went really crazy! We played and played, laughing louder than ever before.
We ended up making a terrible mess — especially me!
My mother kept saying "NEVER AGAIN!"

But you know my mother
completely forgot, and the next week
Jamie and I had a happy time again.

Talk. Talk. Talk.

We just couldn't stop.

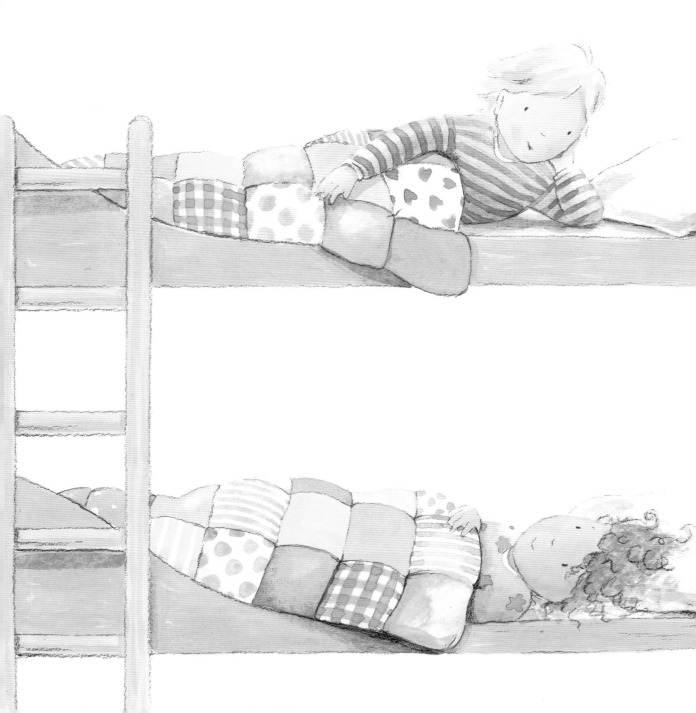

My friend and I are always together
and I'm not lonely anymore.
We'll be friends forever.

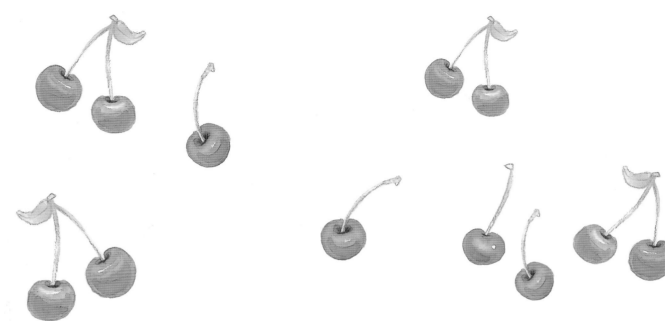

WHAT IS A HELEN EXLEY GIFTBOOK?

Helen Exley Giftbooks cover the most powerful of all human relationships:
the bonds within families and between friends, and the theme of personal values.
No expense is spared in making sure that each book is as meaningful
a gift as it is possible to create: good to give, good to receive.
You have the result in your hands. If you have loved it – tell others!
There is no power on earth like the word-of-mouth recommendation of friends!